For my grandfather, S.H.K., with love
V.F.
For Robert and Chloe
C.V.

First U.S. edition 1993
Published in Great Britain in 1993 by Walker Books Ltd., London.

Library of Congress Cataloging-in-Publication Data

French, Vivian.
Caterpillar, caterpillar / by Vivian French ;
illustrated by Charlotte Voake.—1st U.S. ed.

Summary: A girl learns about caterpillars and butterflies as she
watches her grandfather grow them on the nettles in his garden.
ISBN 1-56402-206-4 (trade) :
1. Caterpillars—juvenile literature. 2. Butterflies—Development—Juvenile literature.
[1. Butterflies. 2. Caterpillars. 3. Metamorphosis.] I. Voake, Charlotte, ill.
II. Title. III. Series: Read and wonder.
QL544.2.F74 1993
595.78'904334—dc20   92-54406

10 9 8 7 6 5 4 3 2 1

Printed in Hong Kong

The pictures for this book were done in
pen and watercolor.

Candlewick Press
2067 Massachusetts Avenue
Cambridge, Massachusetts 02140

CATERPILLAR CATERPILLAR

BY
Vivian French

ILLUSTRATED BY
Charlotte Voake

CANDLEWICK PRESS
CAMBRIDGE, MASSACHUSETTS

My father and my grandfather both liked gardening very much, but my grandfather used to grow stinging nettles. My father didn't; he said they were weeds, and rooted them out.

"Why don't you get rid of your nettles?" I asked my grandfather.

"Stinging nettles grow butterflies," he said. "Go and look."

I went and looked. I couldn't see any butterflies, though. My grandfather turned one of the nettle leaves over to show me the bumps on the back of it, but I didn't know what they were.

"Butterfly eggs," said my grandfather.

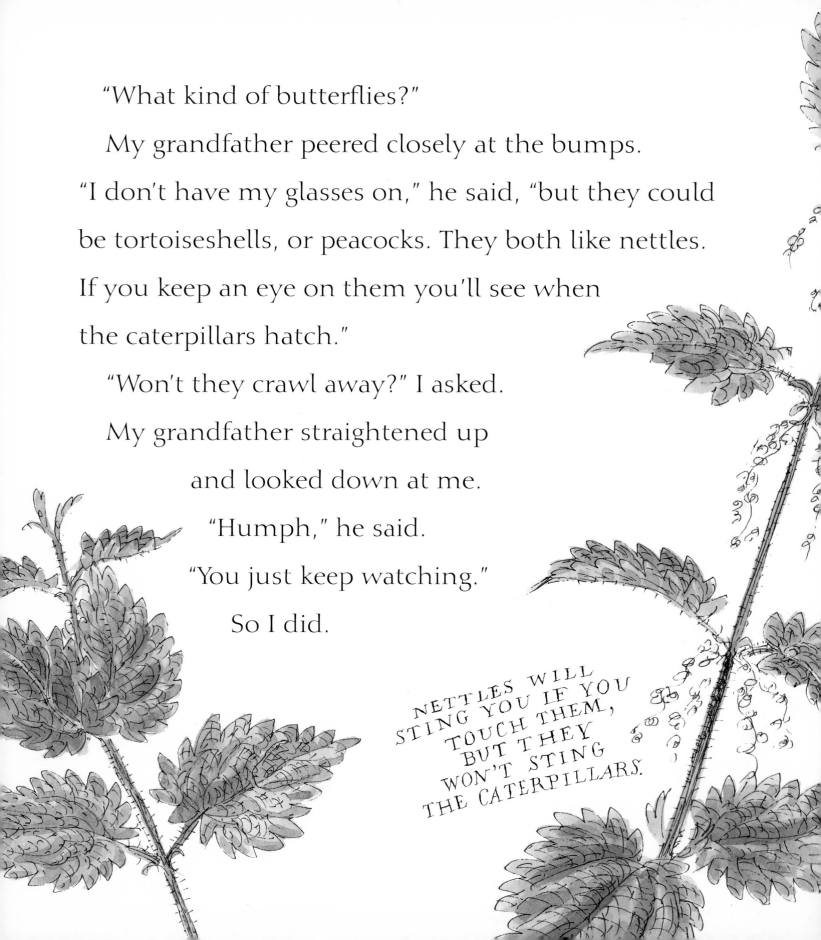

"What kind of butterflies?"

My grandfather peered closely at the bumps.

"I don't have my glasses on," he said, "but they could

be tortoiseshells, or peacocks. They both like nettles.

If you keep an eye on them you'll see when

the caterpillars hatch."

"Won't they crawl away?" I asked.

My grandfather straightened up

and looked down at me.

"Humph," he said.

"You just keep watching."

So I did.

NETTLES WILL
STING YOU IF YOU
TOUCH THEM,
BUT THEY
WON'T STING
THE CATERPILLARS.

THE EGGS ARE
DOME-SHAPED,
WITH LITTLE
RIDGES.
EACH EGG
IS ABOUT THE
SIZE OF THE
TOP
OF A PIN.

MOST
BUTTERFLIES
LAY THEIR EGGS
IN ONES AND TWOS,
MOVING FROM
PLANT TO PLANT.
PEACOCK AND
TORTOISESHELL
BUTTERFLIES
LAY LOTS OF
EGGS AT ONCE.

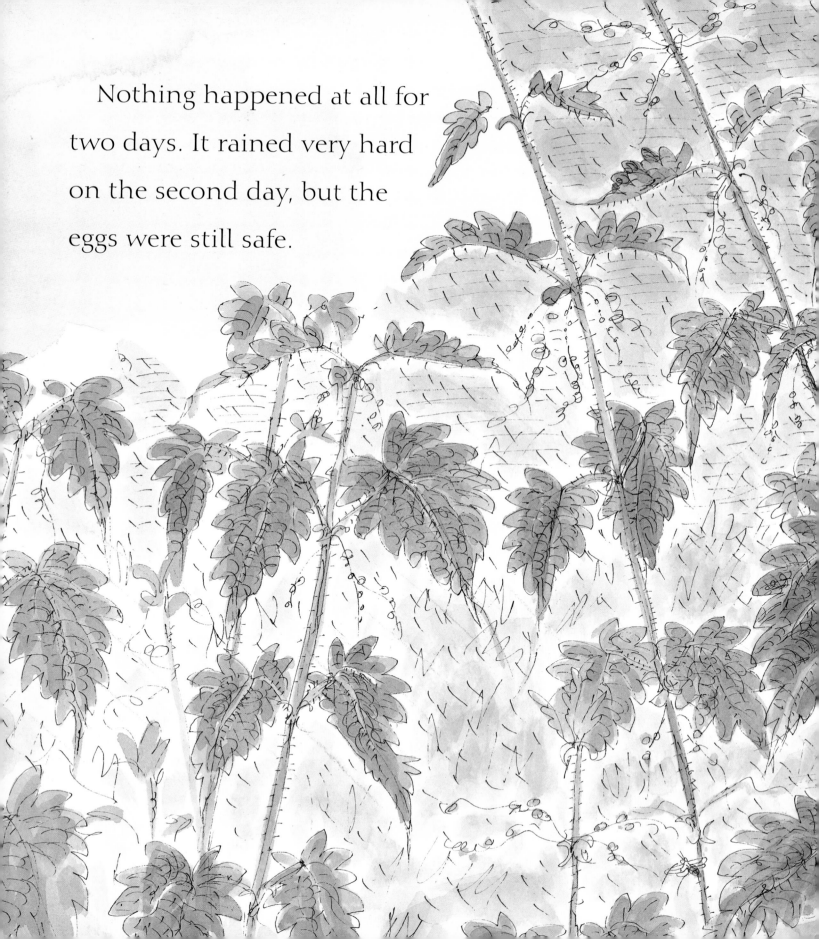

Nothing happened at all for two days. It rained very hard on the second day, but the eggs were still safe.

The next day there were lots and lots of little tiny caterpillars crawling on the nettle leaves. The eggs were papery and empty. I squashed some with my fingernail.

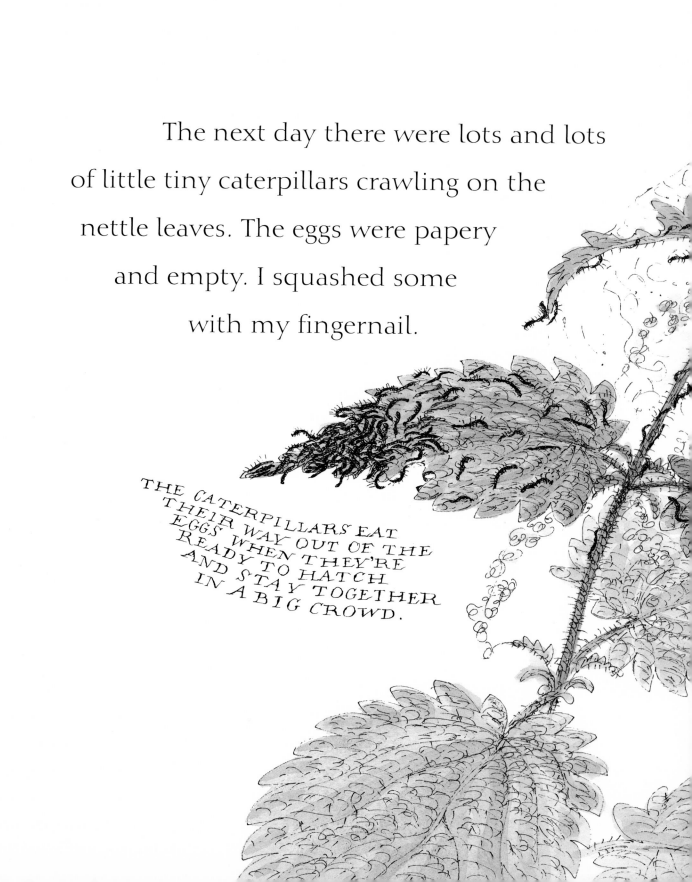

THE CATERPILLARS EAT THEIR WAY OUT OF THE EGGS WHEN THEY'RE READY TO HATCH AND STAY TOGETHER IN A BIG CROWD.

THEY MAKE A WEB OF
WHITE SILK BETWEEN
THE STEM OF THE PLANT
AND THE LEAVES.
IT'S LIKE A TENT.

WHEN THEY'VE EATEN
ALL THE LEAVES NEARBY,
THEY MOVE ON AND
MAKE A NEW TENT

My grandfather came over to see

what I was doing.

"Ah," he said, "peacock caterpillars."

"Do they eat cabbage?" I asked.

I'd seen caterpillars on cabbages.

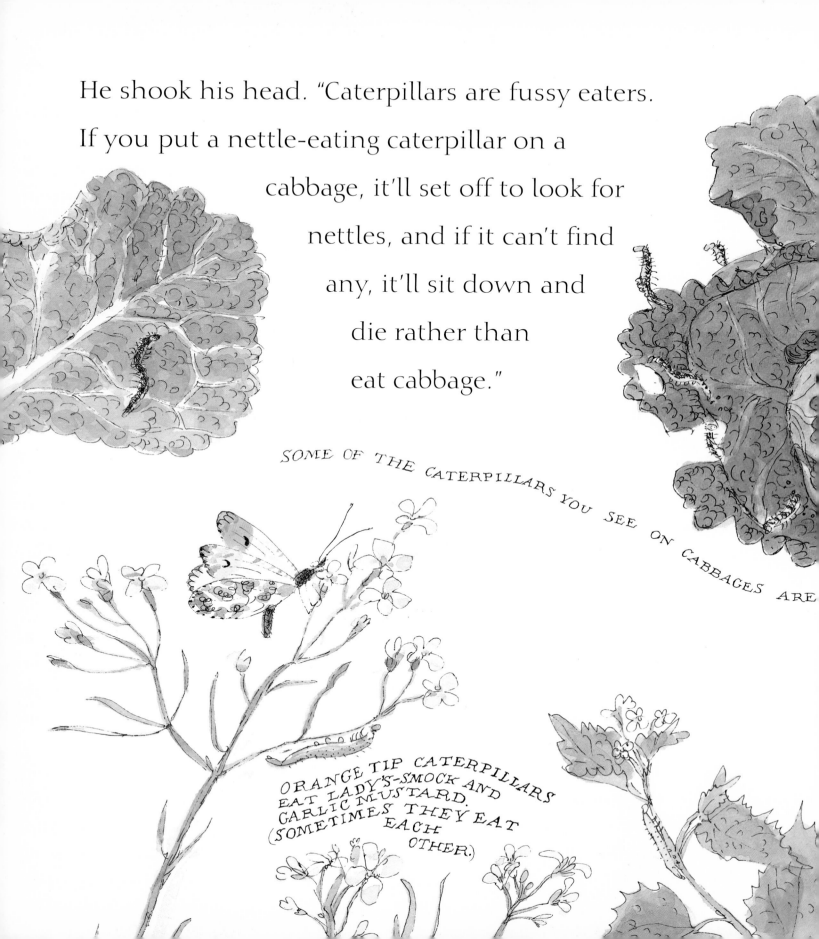

He shook his head. "Caterpillars are fussy eaters. If you put a nettle-eating caterpillar on a cabbage, it'll set off to look for nettles, and if it can't find any, it'll sit down and die rather than eat cabbage."

SOME OF THE CATERPILLARS YOU SEE ON CABBAGES ARE

ORANGE TIP CATERPILLARS EAT LADY'S-SMOCK AND GARLIC MUSTARD. (SOMETIMES THEY EAT EACH OTHER.)

COMMA
CATERPILLARS
LIKE HOPS BEST,
BUT SOMETIMES
THEY HAVE
TO MAKE
DO WITH
NETTLES.

CABBAGE WHITES. THEY LOVE CABBAGE.

PEACOCK,
SMALL TORTOISESHELL,
AND RED ADMIRAL
CATERPILLARS ALL
LIKE NETTLES BEST.

THE CATERPILLARS LEAVE LITTLE DRAVE DROPPINGS WHEREVER THEY GO.

AS THEY GET BIGGER, YOU CAN SEE THEIR WHITE SPOTS MORE CLEARLY.

THEY DON'T MIND WHICH WAY UP THEY EAT, AND THEY HARDLY EVER STOP EATING.

I looked at my peacock caterpillars. They were all together in a little crowd, eating as fast as they could.

"Won't the birds eat them?" I asked. "Couldn't we cover them up?"

"No need," said my grandfather. "Caterpillars that don't hide away are really saying, 'I'm poisonous—keep off!' And the birds know that."

He pulled his pipe out of his pocket and very,
very gently nudged one of the caterpillars.
It curled itself up at once and fell off the leaf.

"There," he said. "Even if something does come along
looking for a snack, the caterpillar might still escape."

"Can I make one curl up?" I stuck my finger out.

"Don't touch them," my grandfather said.

"Some spiny caterpillars can give you a rash,
and other kinds leave a bad smell on
your fingers. Besides, you might hurt them."

THEY HAVE VELVETY BODIES AND SHINY HEADS.
LOOK AT THEIR SPINY BACKS!
THEY HAVE THREE PAIRS OF LEGS
IN FRONT, WITH LITTLE
CLAWS ON THEM, AND
STUMPIER LEGS
FARTHER DOWN.

I went on watching the caterpillars.

They were getting bigger. By the second Saturday in July they had eaten almost all the plant they had hatched on and were crawling over the other nettles.

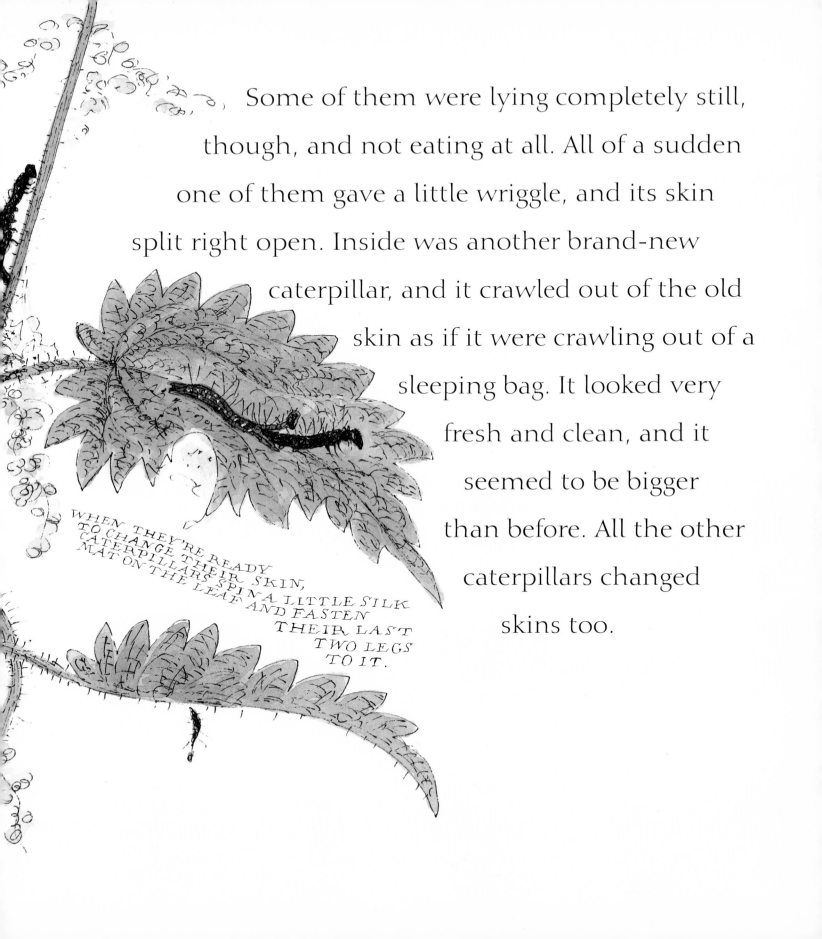

Some of them were lying completely still, though, and not eating at all. All of a sudden one of them gave a little wriggle, and its skin split right open. Inside was another brand-new caterpillar, and it crawled out of the old skin as if it were crawling out of a sleeping bag. It looked very fresh and clean, and it seemed to be bigger than before. All the other caterpillars changed skins too.

WHEN THEY'RE READY TO CHANGE THEIR SKIN, CATERPILLARS SPIN A LITTLE SILK MAT ON THE LEAF AND FASTEN THEIR LAST TWO LEGS TO IT.

I knew something must be eating my caterpillars, because by now there weren't so many of them.

I didn't mind that, but I did mind five days later when I found that every single one of them had disappeared.

"Where have they gone?" I asked. I was close to tears. "Pea sticks," said my grandfather. We marched around the corner of the shed to where the pea sticks were.

"Sometimes one or two come here," my grandfather said.

"Ah, yes, here we are." Sure enough,
there was one of the caterpillars,
hanging head downward off a pea stick.
And to my amazement, before my very
eyes, its skin began to peel off from
its head upward . . . and shrivel away.

This time there wasn't another
caterpillar ready to come out.
Instead there was something
like a little soft brown bag, hanging
on the pea stick. It didn't have legs or eyes or
anything, and it dried up into a little case.

My grandfather said that was just what it was,
but the proper name for it was a pupa or chrysalis.

"But where's the caterpillar gone?" I asked.

All the bits of caterpillar were inside the case,
he said, and they were changing.

WHEN THEY'RE READY TO
PUPATE, THE
CATERPILLARS
LEAVE THEIR
NETTLES.

EACH ONE OF THEM
FINDS A
PLACE TO
BE ON THEIR
OWN.

IT MIGHT BE UP A
TREE, A FENCE,
A STICK, OR A TWIG.

THEY MAKE
A TINY WHITE
PAD...

THEN THEY
ATTACH THEIR
BACK LEGS TO
IT AND HANG
UPSIDE DOWN.

SOON THEIR SKIN PEELS
OFF, LEAVING BEHIND
A BEAUTIFUL PUPA.
IT'S GREEN IF IT'S ON
A LEAF AND BROWN
IF IT'S ON A
TWIG.

Just this once, I was allowed to bring the stick with the little case on it into the kitchen. I watched for ten whole days, and on the tenth day the pupa got very, very dark.

The next morning I was eating my breakfast when my grandfather suddenly said, "LOOK!"

I rushed to see, and the case of the pupa

had split. Something was crawling out . . .

but it didn't look at all like a butterfly.

It was crumpled, and it looked damp,

and it wasn't at all a pretty color.

"It must have gone wrong,"
I said, feeling very sad.

Very gently, my grandfather
lifted the stick and put it on
the windowsill in the sunshine.
The creature crawled slowly up
the stick and stopped.
Little by little it began to stretch out.
It was just like watching a flower
unfolding itself, only it had
wings instead of petals.

THE WINGS
OF THE
BUTTERFLY
UNFOLD AS LIQUID
IS PUMPED INTO
ITS VEINS.

THEY HAVE TO
DRY FOR AN
HOUR OR TWO
BEFORE IT
CAN FLY.

And the wings began to tremble, and to shine in the sunlight, and then suddenly there it was—a real butterfly, with spidery legs, and its wings spread wide open.

It was so lovely that I couldn't say anything at all. Then its wings fluttered and it flew off into the garden—the very newest butterfly there.